Australian Biographical Monographs

3

Australian Biographical Monographs

Series Editor: Scott Prasser

Previous Volumes

1

Joseph Lyons and the Management of Adversity
Kevin Andrews

2

Harold Holt and the Liberal Imagination
Tom Frame

Australian Biographical Monographs
3

Johannes
Bjelke-Petersen

BRUCE KINGSTON

Connor Court Publishing

Published in 2020 by Connor Court Publishing Pty Ltd

Connor Court Publishing Pty Ltd
PO Box 7257
Redland Bay QLD 4165
sales@connorcourt.com
www.connorcourt.com
Phone 0497-900-685

Printed in Australia

ISBN: 9781925826913

Front cover design: Maria Giordano

Front cover picture: Portrait of Sir Johannes Bjelke-Petersen, Queensland
State Archives, circa 1980, public domain.

'Don't you worry about that!

Australian Biographical Monographs

Series Overview

The Connor Court Publishing's Australian Biographical Series on past leading Australian political leaders and other important figures seeks to provide an overview for those who are unfamiliar with the subject and to highlight the person's particular importance, controversies and contributions to Australia's progress.

The monographs are scholarly rather than academic in focus placing emphasis on a clear narrative, but with careful attention to referencing to ensure views expressed are supported by appropriate sources and evidence.

The Series was initiated because of the decline in the study of Australian history at our schools and universities and the consequential lack of knowledge or even worse, distorted views of some of Australia's leading figures who deserve to be remembered, understood for both their achievements, and as each volume also highlights, their flaws.

This monograph by Bruce Kingston on former National Party Queensland Premier Joh Bjelke-Petersen, one of Australia's most well-known state premiers whose impact went beyond the boundaries of his own state that he led from 1968 to 1987 seeks to put his achievements and controversies in context of the time. Bruce, through his work in Queensland Government and other major private sector firms and government agencies when Bjelke-Petersen was at the height of his powers, allows him to provide a real and fresh insight into a premier and his government that is much maligned and often little understood.

- Dr Scott Prasser, May 2020

Johannes Bjelke-Petersen

Bruce Kingston

Perhaps our most maligned, misunderstood and remarkable Premier

In virtually any state in the Commonwealth you could ask any adult in their 40s or above to name a state leader (other than in their residential state) and the majority of them could name Joh – Johannes Bjelke-Petersen, the 31st premier of Queensland and premier from August 1968 until December 1987. You would be hard-pressed to find a state premier who left such an indelible mark on the national psyche. For the purposes of this discussion I will refer to him as 'Joh,' as that is what the vast majority of people knew him as. Of course, if you asked these same people to elucidate on what they remember of Joh, their memories will vary dramatically. Some Queenslanders may talk about a time of strong development and a long period of stability. Many will recall comedian Gerry Connelly impersonations on national TV of a bumbling hick speaking gibberish. Often, they will recite the famed "don't you worry about that" line so closely allied with his media persona. Others, particularly those from southern states will talk of gerrymanders, corruption, white-shoe brigades, civil liberty infringements or daylight savings. And of course, to some extent, all of these would be true. Joh exists in our collective memories as a series of events, a persona like no other, and at times a deeply polarising individual. But too many are quick to dismiss this incredibly successful politician as an aberration of the oddity that is Queensland.

Whether loved or reviled, Johannes Bjelke-Petersen was indeed a polarising figure, but also an indisputably successful one. He was the longest serving and longest-lived premier of Queensland, holding office from 1968 to 1987. He inherited a state that was for much of the time since federation the poor cousin of the Australian states – a backwater or branch-office state known for wool, sugar and minerals, but not much else. Though there had been considerable improvement in Queensland since the Country Party led coalition came to office in 1957, Joh, with his Liberal Party partners, and the support of some highly competent public servants and advisors was going to add considerably to this success in the coming 21 years.

During his time in office he managed the state to become financially sound, attracting capital and immigrants from interstate and internationally and creating a successful economy that has allowed successive governments a good deal of latitude when dealing with their own issues. The Queensland which remained after Joh's passing had a strongly growing population, predominantly into the state's South-East corner, with better levels of education, health and more often than not, employed in a tertiary service sector that was almost unheard of in the early 1960s. All this from a farm boy from Kingaroy with limited education. To understand what drove Joh it is important to understand his formative years.

The formative years

Joh was born in the South Island of New Zealand to Danish immigrant parents though the family relocated to Kingaroy in Queensland when he was only two. His father was a Lutheran pastor and his religious upbringing is in evidence in his policy positions later in life. The Protestant work ethic espousing hard work, discipline, and frugality occur as themes in many of his decisions and battles. His father's ill health brought an end to his formal schooling at 14, with Joh working long hours on the family farm to eke out a meagre living for his family. He convinced the family to take on an additional adjoining property and spent more than a decade living rough on this property in a bark roofed cow bail. The final paragraph of Hugh Lunn's 1978 biography of Joh reads:

> As I stood to leave him, I asked him if the fifteen years alone in a cow bail had taught him much.
> "Yes", he said, "that was a hard life and I learned what you have to do to succeed. Gee whiz, you can learn more in a place like that than at Oxford University. My word you can.[1]

Through this hard work, and with an eye to the future, Joh was eventually able to make a success of peanut farming and land clearing, along the way pioneering a number of methods in both industries. This became a source of capital generation which saw Joh become involved in natural resource exploration, aerial spraying and seeding. Even as he progressed in his pursuits it was not uncommon for him to sleep next to farm machinery in the field so as to have an early start the next day. When he employed staff in his ventures, he would often take the dirtiest or hardest jobs to exemplify his grit and determination. As a successful local identity, in 1946 he was elected to the Kingaroy Shire Council at 35 and at 36 gained the seat of Nanango (later Barambah) representing the then Country Party,[2] which he would hold for the next 40 years. In 1952 he married Florence Gilmour, who was Private Secretary to the Commissioner of Main Roads. After raising four children, Flo as she was most commonly known, assumed a much more significant role in assisting Joh, and eventually went on to become a National Party Senator in her own right, serving as a Queensland Senator for 12 years. In 1963 then Premier Nicklin appointed Joh as Minister for Works and Housing. He recognised early that this portfolio offered many opportunities for him to assist colleagues with government funded construction in their electorates – experience which he was to use to good effect over several years. He was to continue in cabinet until his retirement in 1987.

Queensland is different

Dubbed by some as "the hillbilly dictator"[3] and by Labor Prime Minister Gough Whitlam (1972-75) as a "bible-bashing bastard",[4] too many of Joh's opponents retreated into their cosy metropolitan habitat rather than attempting to understand Queensland. These commentators instead prefer to hide behind this type of epithet rather than coming to grips with the vagaries of Queensland politics and its particular geography and challenges of economic development. It undoubtedly played well to their suburban colleagues but belies a lack of understanding to which Queenslanders have reacted, regularly punishing such views at the ballot box. This was put into sharp focus most recently with the Greens foray during the May 2019 federal election into Queensland pushing their anti-coal agenda, effectively stymying any advance the ALP might have been able to make in many Queensland regional seats. Too often the success of Joh as a public figure and the ongoing success of his governments has been dismissed as an example of the paucity of thought in the average Queenslander. In one reasonably recent article, marking 50 years since Joh became Premier, ex Labor federal Science Minister and an 'Australian Living Treasure' Barry Jones attempted to typify the reasons for Joh's success being his appeal to groups of people he described as:

- Those who look for simple solutions to complex problems

- Those who are apprehensive about the future

- The inarticulate

- Christian fundamentalists

- The lazy and ill-informed

- The white shoe brigade

- Extremists in small business

- The Alf Garnett vote

- People who don't like politics and,

- The smaller government push

His penultimate paragraph perhaps typifies this thinking – "many of us never believed that our relatively liberal democracy could be threatened by an ugly, redneck populism".[5] As even an 'Australian Living Treasure' should be able to understand, the people he disparages above, and who may simply be seen as conservatives when the unnecessary rhetoric is removed, most commonly form the majority of electorates outside inner city metropolitan seats; perhaps explaining the ALP's ongoing lack of success in many non-metropolitan areas, and not just in Queensland. It is perhaps salient to recognise some achievements in Queensland which discredit the 'redneck' and backward epithets:

- Queensland was the first Australian state to abolish capital punishment (1922), and the first government in the Commonwealth to do so;

- The ALP was founded in Queensland, in Barcaldine;

- The current Queensland State Parliament has a female Premier, Deputy Premier and Leader of the Opposition;

- In 1971 Queenslanders saw Australia's first indigenous Senator, Neville Bonner, who was a proud member of the Liberal Party;

- In 1974 Queenslanders elected Eric Deeral, a National Party member, as the first indigenous Australian elected to a State parliament;

- In 1946 Annabelle Rankin, a Liberal Party member, was elected to the Senate, and went on to become the first female federal cabinet minister;

- Queensland's upper House, the Legislative Council, was abolished in 1922, the only state to take such an action;

- Queensland Parliament passed the *Unemployed Workers Insurance Act* in 1922. Queensland was the only Australian state with a scheme to support unemployed workers;

- Free treatment of people in public wards in Queensland public hospitals began in 1945;

- Qantas was founded in 1920 to serve the growing communication and transport needs of the state.

Demographically, Queensland is different to most of the other states in a number of ways. It is easily the most decentralised state in the Commonwealth. No other state has such a decentralised population, with substantial populations almost two thousand kilometres from the State capital, let alone Canberra, Sydney or Melbourne. It is easy to see why Queenslanders may develop a somewhat isolated view. Indeed, most of Queensland's population, lives outside the state capital, Brisbane. By comparison, 65 percent of the NSW population lives in greater Sydney, and Melbourne is home to 76 percent of Victoria's population. Ten of Australia's 30 largest cities are in Queensland. Queensland politics have often produced results unlikely in other states. Prior to World War One, the labour movement was so militant in regional Queensland that is was dubbed 'the Red North.' During this time, a radical Labor government led by Premier T J Ryan created state enterprises in direct competition with commercial business. At its peak the Queensland Government under Labor, was running a cannery, a sawmill, a state hotel, a state sugar mill, mines and smelters, and state cattle stations and butcheries. By the 1930s there were major and often violent strikes in the north, often led by Communist Party militants. In fact, the only Communist ever elected to an Australian Parliament, Fred Paterson was elected in 1944 for the state seat of Bowen. The highly decentralised nature and agricultural base of the state economy combined with low rates of industrialisation has meant that Queensland traditionally has a much more diminished local pool of capital to draw upon. Apart from a few stand-out examples, foreign and southern companies had dominated the commercial landscape and it could be said that this meant that the government became responsible for driving investment and development. This is one thing Joh understood very well.

Understanding the voter's mood

– the need for strong leadership

Just as Whitlam and the Labor Party undoubtedly understood the mood of the Australian electorate with their 'It's Time' campaign in 1972, sweeping them to power after 23 years of Coalition governments, Joh exhibited a similar masterful understanding of his local voting public. He understood that many in his state wanted certainty, employment, and were inherently conservative. They also liked strong, direct leaders. These were Joh's people and as can be seen in numerous election results, even those who could be considered to be rusted-on Labor voters, such as many blue-collar workers, would vote for Joh again and again, even if voting ALP in other levels of government.

He was also apparently able to clearly see that militancy and sectional self-interest, either exhibited by striking electricity workers or by university students marching in the streets did not sit well with the bulk of the Queensland voting public. Street marches and their predecessor, the Springbok riots, were an early example of this. Quite apart from the issue of apartheid, the 1971 Springbok tour of Australia presented Joh with an excellent opportunity to again exhibit strength of leadership to the general community. Due to the violence seen in other states, a State of Emergency was declared, and additional police were brought in from across the State. Much has been written of the events surrounding the 'riots' around the Tower Mill Hotel and while protestors may have believed that they had been unfairly and violently targeted by the police in attendance, the bulk of the reporting of the incidents played directly to Joh's people, showing an unruly mob attempting to disrupt a public event. In the following years, Joh was similarly able to use the illegal street marches as a stalking horse of sorts, enabling him to pitch the unruly behaviour of 'scruffy, long-haired layabouts' against people attempting to go about their normal business. He baited the hook with statements like 'the day of the political street march is over'[6] and the march organisers could not help but take the bait. Time and again marchers, whether from a university or civil liberties groups, were met with strong police action – often just in time for the evening news.

In the mid-1980s, Queensland was experiencing ongoing power problems brought about by strikes and rolling stoppages by unions in the power industry. After one particularly bad late afternoon summer storm in January 1985, some quarter of a million Queenslanders were without power yet only limited actions by the State Emergency Service (SES) could be taken to remedy the situation. The Electrical Trades Union (ETU) was on strike and union officials steadfastly refused to allow or permit their members to return to work. At an emergency sitting of the Industrial Commission they were ordered to return to work and the union agreed, belatedly and under duress, to restore power some six hrs after the storm's onset. While there had been increasing industrial disputation in the industry during the early 1980s, this marked the start of a major campaign of power disruption which saw 1,000 electricity workers striking in early February of that year. On 7 February 1985, after ongoing and increasingly ineffectual processes by the State Industrial Commission, Joh declared a State of Emergency and withdrew the electricity industry from the jurisdiction of the Commission. This 'line in the sand' created a clear demarcation and another possibility for the Premier to be seen as a strong leader willing to fight for the comfort and lifestyle of the average Queenslander.

By giving the striking workers an ultimatum to return to work, (which most of them rejected) Joh immediately progressed to sacking the striking workers and commencing the process of employing new staff on contracts to keep the power on. A period of rolling blackouts ensued throughout the state, exacerbated by 'sympathy' industrial actions by a number of other unions and an organised process of harassment of the South East Queensland Electricity Board (SEQEB) employees by sacked and striking workers. As the tensions increased, the intensity of the harassment escalated, as described by the SEQEB General Manager, Wayne Gilbert, at the time:

> Those employees that dismissed themselves embarked on a role of extreme harassment. ... A number of men were working at Fisherman's Island up a pole between energised mains at 33,000 volts. Along came a group of harassers (about 20). They interfered with the work that was proceeding on the ground, threatened people working in the air... Threats were also made along the lines of 'When you are at work, who is protecting your wife and kids?' ... 'When we come back to work you will never be safe. You might think you are working on dead mains, and somebody's going to throw the switch and fry you alive'... Cars have been vandalized, windows broken, and countless abusive and obscene telephone calls directed at workers' families.[7]

Even as SEQEB began to employ new staff, further blackouts were caused by some 200 members of a different union forcing power stations to limit their supply. Joh recognised that this militancy and extreme harassment was completely unacceptable to the general public and successfully turned the bulk of Queenslanders against them. The Petersen Government even advertised the name and addresses of these unionists in the press, encouraging Queenslanders to let them know how they felt. In Parliament in early 1985 Joh's Minister for Mines and Energy, Ivan Gibbs, was able to succinctly support his point with the comment, "Queenslanders have a right to expect a reliable and continuous electricity supply. It is not the right of a handful of union bosses to decide when in excess of two million Queenslanders can turn on the lights, switch on any electrical appliance of their own choosing or earn a living dependent on electricity".[8]

The dispute was also useful to Joh in allowing him to corral the state Labor parliamentary opposition into an unfavorable position of neither wishing to condemn the striking workers outright nor wanting to support the government's action to resolve the dispute. Speaking to a parliamentary motion regarding the dispute being put by the Premier, Joh 's capacity to be equally humorous and taunting to the ALP is exhibited:

> The motion requires the Leader of the Opposition

and his colleagues to end their fence-sitting on the vital question of obedience to orders issued by the Industrial Commission. It is a barbed-wire fence and so far, the Leader of the Opposition has been trying to walk along it with one foot on either side. If that spectacle can be pictured in one's mind's eye, it would not be hard to visualise the inherent dangers of such a stance.[9]

The Labor parliamentary wing was thus unable to take a clear stand during these events, making 'fudging' statements referring to recognising the rights of the workers, but also the need for a consistent power supply. Even leading into an election year with the two conservative parties sniping at each other, the ALP was unable to make any headway, losing two more seats in the November 1986 poll. While this dispute was said to have cost the Queensland economy some $600 million, the long-term positive effects for SEQEB were substantial. SEQEB General Manager, Wayne Gilbert noted that annualised savings of at least $37 million per annum would accrue thanks to modernised labour practices. Moreover, he added that "since SEQEB's inception some eight years ago, there was an average of 30,000 manhours lost each year due to strikes, at a cost of $500,000 per annum. That figure, I am pleased to inform you, has now been reduced to zero".[10]

It should also be noted that in this latter period of his

government, Joh's strong leadership bringing into focus as it did the paucity of Labor leadership, also probably served to bring the Liberal's poor performance into sharp focus in the electorates mind. Undoubtedly, while Joh recognised that the benefits from these modernised labour practices would eventually accrue across the Queensland economy, he was probably unaware that he had accidentally stumbled on micro-economic reform – the very policy that the Hawke-Keating federal government was pursuing at the same time to make the Australian economy more competitive.

The Gerrymander

– A convenient excuse for defeat

"While it is true that the Queensland electoral boundaries were malapportioned between 1949 and 1992, it was the second preferences, first of the Democratic Labor Party and then the Liberal Party, that sustained Country-Liberal coalitions in 1957-1983 and then National Party governments from 1983-89. When, for the first time since 1956, the ALP achieved a majority of the two-party preferred vote in 1989, it won government in a landslide – despite the existence of the so-called 'Bjelkemander'".[11]

Throughout the 1960s and 1970s the so-called 'gerrymander' (or more correctly in this case technically a malapportionment) of the Queensland electoral boundaries was most commonly used as the main explanation that the ALP was unsuccessful in its many bids to become the state's government. To this day, it is regularly trotted out by journalists and academics alike as a prime example of the type of corruption to which we poor Queensland voters were subjected. Although as you can see from the above quote, the reality was far from this 'truth', even admitted as it is in a far from positive article about Joh. As recently as 2014, it was still being relied upon as 'proof', with the gerrymander being quoted as a prime cause of Labor's ongoing poor election results:

> … Joh Bjelke-Petersen's electoral gerrymanders which famously kept Labor out of power for 32 years in that state. However, in the Australian political landscape, Joh's gerrymander, although long lasting, was unusual and considered pretty scandalous.[12]

As the late Professor Colin Hughes commented, "few aspects of Queensland politics have attracted more attention and more hostile criticism than the State's electoral system, yet in the main it differs little from that of the four other mainland states".[13]

Historically, all governments, to a lesser or greater extent, have modified voting systems with an eye to their own success and with a view to 'fairness' as it exists in their perspective. It has only been a relatively recent development which has seen the drawing of electoral boundaries by reasonably independent bodies. In countries as vast as Australia, the difficulties of standardising voter numbers in electorates while also taking into account their physical size has been a troubling one since the early 1900s. While small inner-city seats may be easily and quickly traversed in an Uber, an elected representative in a large Queensland seat will be facing the challenges of an electorate thousands of square miles in size and having few communication and transport methods available. This was particularly crucial prior to modern communication methods and it is only relatively recently that Queenslanders in remote locations have had access to reliable internet to allow fast and regular communication with their politicians. Up until the years immediately post World War Two, many outback centres could only be reached by train, or horse and buggy with a regular, though somewhat unreliable mail service.

In 1942 the Queensland Labor Government introduced the plurality (or first past the post) system of voting seeking to divide the opposition party votes. In 1949 the Hanlon Labor Government divided the state into three zones, metropolitan, provincial cities and rural. Each seat within a zone had roughly the same number of voters, but the voter numbers allowed in each zone varied substantially. This saw remote seats with as few as 5,000 voters and metropolitan seats with as many as 25,000 – a 5 to 1 variation between the largest and smallest seats. But even with this system expressly developed to 'protect' their position, after the disastrous split in the Labor Party in the 1957, the ALP was reduced to only 31 seats and was to remain out of office until 1989 not reaching the needed 50 per cent of two-party preferred (TPP) votes until that point. The truth of the situation is that the Country-Liberal Coalition when it came to office in 1957 after being in opposition since 1932, inherited from Labor the 'gerrymander' or malapportionment electoral system, which had been created prior to the 1950 state election to protect Labor's seats in provincial cities and to a lesser extent rural areas and thus hold onto power. This was most obvious in the results of the 1950 state election where the Hanlon Labor Government won 45 seats (out of a 75 seat chamber) with 46.9 per cent of the vote while the Country-Liberal Coalition with 49.2 per cent of the vote gained only 31 seats, though not dissimilar results are found in the preceding two decades. Substantial movements in mechanisation and the population drift to cities and towns accelerated the changes in voter enrolment which would eventually see these 'safe' ALP areas turn towards the Coalition.

During Joh's premiership, the electoral system was further modified with an additional zone, and all zones were renamed. They became: the Western and

Far Northern Zone; the Country Zone; the Provincial Cities Zone; and the South Eastern Zone. In 1986 the difference between the smallest seat of Warrego (some 8,000 voters) and the largest seat of Fassifern (some 32,000 voters) showed a 4 to 1 variation. Sir Robert Sparkes, long-time the President of the Country Party, and then National Party President (1970-90), explained his party's view of the electoral system in a Queensland Press Club speech in 1981 where he said, "The basis of the electoral system applied by successive Queensland governments since 1957, is that every Queenslander, no matter where he or she lives, is entitled to adequate and effective representation, and that cannot be achieved by a strict one-vote, one-value distribution of electorates".[14] Separately he also stated, "If the National Party wanted to make a song and dance about it, then it could justifiably claim to be disadvantaged by the present system of electoral boundaries – at BOTH ends of the scale".

It is interesting to note that during the late 1970s and into the 1980s the National Party held not only the smallest, least populated seats in the state, but also some of the largest, undermining critics and their argument of the one vote, one value. It should also be pointed out that a Labor government was elected in Western Australia with a far larger difference in seat sizes than exists in Queensland. Indeed, even as late 1979, the then Queensland Labor Opposition Leader, Ed Casey was advocating a system with two zones, West and Far North, and Coastal, effectively agreeing that some form of electoral weightage was needed. There is certainly little or no evidence to suggest in the elections during Joh's premiership, that the 'gerrymander' would have substantially changed election outcomes. The size of the swing at the 1974 state election (even with more favourable electorate sizes) meant that few (if any) ALP members would have been saved from losing. The ALP received only 36 per cent of the vote even though they contested all 82 seats, while the Nationals received 28 per cent of the vote contesting only 48 seats. Overall, the Coalition received almost 59 per cent of the vote. Similarly, in the 1977 and 1980 elections there is little evidence to support the view that the ALP was excluded from office by the 'gerrymander' as they received 42.8 per cent of the vote in 1977 and 41.5 per cent in 1980, while again contesting all seats.

Some form of electoral weighting exists in many democracies across the world usually as they attempt to ensure that less populated areas have some form of reasonably equal representation against the more populace regions. Even in today's Commonwealth Parliament (generally not said to be malapportioned or gerrymandered), seats range in size from Lingiari in the Northern Territory with 65,752 voters to Canberra with 144,931 voters. And of course, the most obvious form of electoral weighting in Australia exists today in the Australian Senate where some 5.2 million electors in NSW elect 12 Senators as do the .38 million electors in Tasmania. And yet the .29 million electors in the ACT elect only two Senators. No accusation of gerrymander is raised and yet the issue of 'one vote, one value' so championed by the Liberal and Labor parties is flagrantly flaunted. This is perhaps the reason for Prime Minister Paul Keating's famously calling senators "unrepresentative swill".[15]

A prominent argument regarding the 'gerrymander' suggests that Joh was premier with only 39 per cent of the primary vote (1983 figures) and that he did not deserve the premiership as Labor achieved a 44 per cent vote. This argument actively, and in all likelihood intentionally, ignores the fact that the National Party (and before that the Country Party) governed in coalition with the support of the Liberal Party, which in 1983 achieved a 15 per cent vote. This converted to a 1983 two-party preferred total of 53.4 per cent vs 46.6 per cent for Labor – still a clear loss for the ALP. Even in the 1972 state election where Labor gained 46.8 per cent of the vote standing in all 82 seats, the Country Party received 20 per cent of the vote standing candidates in only 44 seats. Their Coalition partner, the Liberals, gained 22.2 per cent standing in 53 seats. In three seats there were no Coalition candidates at all. Meanwhile, the Democratic Labor

Party (DLP) gained 7.7 per cent (heavily preferenced to the Coalition candidates) standing in 72 seats. This form of lazy analysis also too easily ignores the fact that while the Labor usually fielded a candidate in every seat, thereby naturally increasing their percentage of the overall state vote, the Nationals (again in 1983 figures) stood candidates in only 72 seats. Indeed, it is not unreasonable to suggest that had the Nationals stood in all 82 seats, they not only would have gained as high a vote as Labor, but that by running in the remaining Liberal seats they may well have removed all except one or two Liberals, effectively removing them from politics in Queensland. This undermines Labor's claim that they were prevented from gaining the required number of seats to form government and would have dealt an even more serious blow to the morale of Labor.

It was not only the ALP that continued the 'gerrymander' arguments in state politics. Throughout the 1970s and 1980s there were regular calls by Liberal Party state conferences for a more 'equitable distribution of seats.' Proposals varied widely, with some recognising zonal systems, others for strict one-vote, one-value systems though occasionally with 20 per cent margins instead of the usual 10 per cent. It is important to note that while so many groups clambered for a so-called 'fairer' system under a one-vote, one value system, they were often failing to recognise the real electoral facts behind the rhetoric. In 1981 the Queensland Liberal Party Secretariat carried out a computer analysis assessing the effect of a one-vote, one-value system redistribution on the 1980 voting figures. This projection showed that the Nationals would have gained 29 seats, the Liberals 25 seats and the ALP 28 seats. This would have had the Nationals with a four-seat lead over the Liberals and a completely clear Coalition majority over Labor with a seat count of 54 to 28. A far cry from the actual outcome of Nationals 41, Labor 32 and Liberals 8 but not a different outcome for Labor in real terms.

Simply put, the 'gerrymander' myth that Labor, many journalists and most academics have used to excuse the poor performance of the Labor Opposition under Joh is just another example of the paucity of intellectual scrutiny too often applied to Queensland politics and a lack of sound and rigorous analysis and understanding of the complexities of the electoral system.

The Queensland Economy under Joh

– from economic Cinderella to economic powerhouse

For the Coalition which came to power in 1957 and inherited an impoverished economy, the promotion of development and investment in Queensland were crucial to modernise the state, create jobs, especially in regional Queensland, and to ensure Queensland was less dependent on Commonwealth funding with their ever-increasing conditions. While considerable progress had been made since the Coalition came to power under Premier Nicklin (1957-1968), this focus was to increase considerably during the Bjelke-Petersen years. It was helped by competent Liberal treasurers, especially Sir Gordon Chalk (Treasurer from 1965 to 1976) and a professional public service.

During Joh's time in office, he was said to be most proud of the building of the Wivenhoe and Burdekin dams, the Gateway Bridge, the electrification and modernisation of the rail network – including the Brisbane suburban lines, hosting the Commonwealth Games in 1982 and the success of World Expo 1988. But just as important as these big-ticket developments were his championing of the abolition of state death duties (against the advice of his then Liberal Treasurer) and the extension of stamp duty concessions and exemptions to small business, family property transfer, first home buyers and mortgages. This caused a large influx of retirees into Queensland. Additionally, he introduced payroll tax exemptions for small businesses and employers with apprentices – all aimed at cementing the position of Queensland as the "low tax state." He has been dubbed "the father of the Queensland tourism industry," developing airports across the state and tourism precincts which continue to this day. In just ten years from the late 1950s, Australia had moved from being a coal importing nation to becoming a major coal exporting nation. Only another ten years after that saw it become one of the largest coal suppliers in the world, and Queensland had the bulk of that business. The construction of major ports such as Gladstone (at one stage the largest coal terminal in the world and a significant aluminium producer) and the development of new power stations throughout the state meant that the production of aluminium almost doubled. Bob Katter, one time state Country Party member and minister, and now a federal parliamentarian for the Katter Australia Party, dubbed this period as the "great flowering of developmentalism" and further noted that "... until the late 1980s, (Joh) signalled that Queensland was open for business and led to the emergence of a modern, sophisticated state in Australia's north".[16]

This of course drove a considerable portion of the Australian economy at the time as many of these developments took quite some years to bear fruit for the Queensland economy. In the years following Joh's departure the growth in the gross state product of Queensland outperformed that of all the other states and territories. In that period Queensland's gross domestic product (GDP) grew 5.0 per cent each year, while growth in Australia's national GDP rose on average 3.9 per cent each year. Queensland's contribution to the Australian GDP increased by 10.4 per cent in that period, one of only three states to do so. Joh famously noted how successful Brisbane was looking because of the number of cranes on the skyline. One can debate the aesthetics of various buildings constructed during this period, but what cannot be debated was the level of income and employment such projects generated.

Tourism developments were another major focus of Joh's government with major projects taking place at or around Cairns, Townsville, the Whitsundays, Mackay, the Sunshine Coast and of course the Gold Coast. These were driven by numerous airport developments as well as major hotel and infrastructure projects. Notable among these were Queensland's casino. With Joh a lay Lutheran preacher and Sir Llew Edwards, the Liberal State Treasurer (1978-1983) the son of a Congregationalist Minister the drivers of these developments were initially stymied. However, both eventually accepted the commercial arguments put forward and Sir Llew in particular, set about creating an environment whereby Queensland had some of the toughest casino legislation in the world. While so often a magnet for organised crime and money laundering, the legislation and accompanying tender process intrinsically excluded a number of potential tenderers because of their known or likely organised crime connections. The eventual winning tenderer was

Jennings Industries. Initially, this was seen by some as another contract for a National Party mate. However, the reality of the situation was that the original long list of potential tenderers was substantially reduced by careful police and public service scrutiny leaving a local major construction company with the contract. There was criticism by some in the tourism industry that the eventual casinos were not as exciting as their Las Vegas counterparts, but the need for removing the criminal taint so often associated with that glitter city's developments was placed above the 'excitement factor' of the developments.

Developmentalism and corruption

It is almost impossible to consider Joh's premiership without the issue of corruption being raised whether or not discussion is based on evidence or just hearsay. Chris Master's ABC 4 Corners program, *The Moonlight State*[17] and earlier exposes by local journalist, Phil Dickie[18] ensured that all Australia knew of a festering level of Queensland police corruption involving drugs, prostitution and gambling. Critics have often delighted in portraying Queensland as a 'police state,' or as an inordinately corrupt one, but neither position survives the level of attention that it has received – at least when seen in comparison to most other Australian states and territories. Of course, some corruption in various forms is endemic in virtually all modern police systems – those in New South Wales, Victoria, South Australia, Western Australia would be hard pressed to point a finger at Queensland while ignoring the endemic corruption either in their police or certain public enterprises. Some states (notably NSW and Victoria) have had such endemic police and political corruption (as numerous royal commissions testify)[19] that popular television shows have been created portraying only thinly veiled (or sometimes explicitly) characters of serving police officers and politicians. At the same time, corruption in some state governments such as Western Australia, caused massive misallocations of public funding costing hundreds of millions of dollars in dodgy deals with questionable businesses and entrepreneurs with little or any tangible benefits to state taxpayers. This may have simply been incompetent though the state government in question assured the public that this was an appropriate use of government funds. It follows then that if they are to be believed then corruption seems a more logical answer for such inappropriate funding.[20]

Indeed, it has been said that one of the things that typified Joh's Queensland was that if there was corruption, it usually resulted in the construction of a hospital, dam, railway, bridge or other piece of public infrastructure. As opposed to the corruption most often identified with the other side of politics commonly involving a crony being placed in a high paying government job or an exchange of money with little or no actual public benefit. There were statements made during the Fitzgerald Inquiry[21] regarding large sums of cash being delivered in brown paper bags to the Executive Building[22] from major national and international developers. Joh admitted this, but also stated that the funds were immediately transferred to National Party coffers for use in election campaigns.

The issue of over-riding individual local governments to ensure large scale developments proceed had also often been misconstrued as a corrupt use of ministerial power while on balance it can be seen as a practical approach to promoting large scale development in various regions.

Sadly, all sides of politics have individual politicians whose individual moral compasses allow them to personally enrich their bank accounts. Joh's cabinet was undoubtedly no different. Some senior cabinet members were renowned for championing the cause of developers and casino operators though interestingly while gossip and hearsay to this effect abounds, neither courts nor commissions of inquiry ever found more than relatively minor corruption (travel entitlements for instance in the case of the Fitzgerald Inquiry)[23] among Joh's ministerial colleagues. You have to look at Labor governments preceding the Country Party[24] and those after 1986 to find ministers forced to resign because of impropriety and corruption. Indeed, it was Gordon Nuttall, who was minister in the Beattie Labor Government, who served prison time for receiving corrupt payments from a mining company.

In discussion with a number of people who knew and/ or worked with Joh, the overwhelming view seems to be that Joh had a type of market fundamentalism which potentially allowed a level of corruption in his cohort in exchange for loyalty and perceived tangible benefits to the state. 'Perceived' is stressed here, as the Country (now National) Party, and to a lesser extent the Liberal Party, commonly exhibited an "all development is good development" view of the state which meant that there was not always a strategic approach to development proposals and indeed some poorly conceived developments are still apparent throughout the state.

Public service
- Interference and corruption or implementing merit and efficiencies

As noted in an *Age* article by an academic from 2005 disparagingly titled "Sir Joh, our home-grown banana republican" published just after his death, the author stated that "the upper ranks of the public service were politicised for party advantage".[25] Yet when studied more closely the period of Joh's premiership saw a remarkable stability of senior public service figures. It has been said by many contemporaries of Joh that the likes of the Under Treasurer, the Head of the Public Service and the Co-Ordinator General were some of the only people who could say 'no' to Joh's face and get away with it. Many senior public service figures remained in office throughout his premiership, a far cry from today's post-election period when there is often wholesale replacement of most, if not all, department heads and senior staff with political appointees and 'of the faith' ministerial staff who completely blur the lines of providing independent advice. 'Frank and fearless' advice existed under Joh, perhaps one of the last times it occurred in Queensland and Australia, given the development of the 'responsive' public service across all jurisdictions since the 1980s.

As noted by former Australian Treasury official, Gene Tunny referring to Under Treasurer Sir Leo Hielscher in his recent book on Queensland Government finances, "Sir Leo was the last Under Treasurer to serve under the old Whitehall model of permanent departmental heads, a model which gave public servants considerable authority in their dealings with Ministers…".[26] He added "Up until at least the late 1980s in Queensland, it appears public servants could stand their ground with ministers and play a huge role in decision making owing to their strengths vis-a-vis ministers".[27]

What could be portrayed by some as interfering in the independence of the public service could also be more correctly typified as streamlining and seeking efficiencies. The removal of public servants from the old industrial processes they had enjoyed previously had more to do with Joh's desire to emasculate unions and their processes of embedding overmanning and 'feather-bedding' as it had to do with public service control. It also had a lot to do with a philosophical position of limiting the growth and impact of the public service to allow free enterprise to flourish. While some may typify the removal of some career service conventions as politicising the public service, it could equally be argued that this was done to remove inherent inefficiencies that militated against moves to creating a more merit-based service. Many aspects of the historical Queensland Public Service were based upon seniority and not merit. Even when the National Party Government enacted new legislation that strengthened merit and with new promotion criteria of superior efficiency or equal efficiency and merit, permanent heads of departments in reality controlled most promotion decisions and generally relied upon traditional seniority considerations:

> This government (National Party) also escalated intervention in industrial matters from 1983 to 1987. It refused to negotiate pay claims, but cut conditions such as leave loading and flexible working hours. It

> removed union preference for public employees and
> refused payroll deductions for union membership
> fees.[28]

The above quote is given as an example of negative political influence on the public service, but when the polemic is ignored, these types of actions are simply an extension of Joh's ongoing emphasis on freeing the public service from what it saw as an insidious and highly restrictive union stranglehold. Following a more free market principle, Joh did not think it was appropriate for employees to be 'forced' either directly or indirectly into membership of an organisation with direct links to the Labor. During these periods, there were also strong religious groupings within individual departments which meant that promotions within these 'cliques' were made on less than the normal performance and aptitude standards. A number of high profile industrial disputes of the late 1970s and early 1980s saw dramatic intervention by Joh in industrial relations, but again this had little if anything to do with a supposed desire to interfere in the public service per se, but was focussed more on breaking the power of individual unions. Joh made it very clear on many occasions that he felt the shackles of enforced unionism were inappropriate in this day and age and were burdensome to the Queensland economy.

This undoubtedly has been seen as 'interfering' or

'corrupt' by those on the left of politics, and yet was roundly applauded by the general populace and roundly rewarded at upcoming elections by the voters. It should also be noted that some 'interference' in public service practices could rather be seen as modernising the public service and therefore moving with the times. As Linda Colley noted:

> In 1932 the (Labor) government further restricted women's employment to clerk-typists rather than clerks, exacerbating occupational segregation with no disagreement from public sector unions. Appeal processes continued to defend seniority albeit not for women.[29]

While Colley also noted that under the Coalition "opportunities for women to compete on their merits increased greatly with the removal of the marriage bar in 1969 and access to jobs as clerks (rather than just clerk- typists) in 1972 ...".[30] Another issue which should be mentioned here is the 'soft inherent corruption' of Labor staff and or defeated Members getting 'looked after', either in Queensland public service roles or in convenient posts in like-minded governments in Sydney, Melbourne or Canberra ensuring they learn useful skills before they enter the corridors of power. The Coalition parties on the other hand, have always been less adept at sponsoring staff into training or developmental roles, preferring to bring in outsiders for a 'fresh set of eyes' often to the detriment of their policy management capacity. One only has to look at the Labor administration following the demise of National Party government in 1989 (eg the Goss Labor Government 1989-1996) to see the increase in political interference in the senior ranks of the public service. This commenced a process of turning most senior roles in the public service into contract roles, with senior staff moved in and out of roles at the whim of political decision makers. It is a practice that has now been emulated by subsequent non-Labor governments in Queensland – the Borbidge and Newman Coalition governments. This contractualising and use of lateral appointments of those from outside the normal ranks of the public service at all levels of government has undoubtedly done more damage to the Whitehall system of 'frank and fearless advice' than ever occurred during the Joh era, creating an environment where even those outside the direct realms of political influence have to second guess their political masters to safeguard their careers.

Electoral Success

– bringing the fight to Whitlam and the ALP

It could be said that the election of a national Labor government in 1972 was a godsend to Joh. From its inception as a duumvirate – only Gough Whitlam and Lance Barnard were initially sworn in as government ministers and held 27 portfolios between them – changes came thick and fast. The speed and volume of changes, while many were politically not very significant, caused disquiet in many circles. Additionally, bungles such as a raid on ASIO (ordered by the Attorney General, Senator Lionel Murphy), disagreements with various state governments and Whitlam's failed attempt via referendum to move control of wages and prices to the Commonwealth made them easy pickings for Joh. Added to this, the Whitlam Government's 1973-74 Federal Budget which massively increased spending and focussed more on social welfare objectives rather than on measures needed to restore the economy, control spending, reduce inflation and be seen to tackle the growing unemployment that Australia was suffering from at this time. As the *Age* later commented:

> As the Whitlam Government pressed on with its big-spending reforms despite Treasury pleas for restraint, Commonwealth spending surged 46 per cent in 1974-75, dwarfing the 20 per cent rise the year

before. It was the year the Australian economy went bung. It began with unemployment at 2 per cent but ended with it heading for 5 per cent. A generation of jobs for everyone was over. It was the year wages and prices soared out of control. Consumer prices rose 16 per cent, yet wages topped that, rising 28 per cent as powerful unions came back for a second or even a third round of pay rises.[31]

What has now become known, thanks to Wikileaks sources, is that the United States Embassy was compiling information, much of it gleaned from ALP sources, regarding the looming crises the Whitlam Government was facing:

> Senior public servants complained about chronic leaks of information to the media from ministers, ill-disciplined political staff and disgruntled bureaucrats. Although Labor won the May 1974 double dissolution election, some of Whitlam's closest confidants were quick to brief the embassy on growing paralysis and gloom within the government. The embassy correctly identified the Khemlani loans scandal and the resignation of minerals and energy minister Rex Connor as the trigger for the final political and constitutional crisis that engulfed the government.[32]

All of this was wonderful grist for the mill for Joh

who was quick to lay virtually any economic or social negative at the feet of Canberra. Always alert to perceived encroachments by the Whitlam Government into states' areas of control, Joh was quick to recognise his chance with the 'Gair Affair' to thwart its intrusions. In early 1974, with no control over a Senate which was stymying his legislative program, Whitlam hatched a plan to improve their chance of a Senate majority at the next election. He offered the post of Ambassador to Ireland to an ex ALP Premier and now DLP senator from Queensland, Vince Gair.

In what was dubbed "The Night of the Long Prawns," Whitlam's plan was scuttled by Joh who was informed that if he could have the Queensland Governor issue writs prior to Gair's resignation from the Senate for only five rather than six senate seats in Queensland then the loss of Gair would be nullified. While Gair was kept occupied by National Party senators with a beer and prawn dinner, the deadline for him to resign passed and Joh convinced his Cabinet to advise the Queensland Governor to issue writs for only five senators. This happened, and while there was substantial debate in the Commonwealth Parliament on the move in the following weeks, the matter was overtaken by events when Whitlam called a double dissolution election on 10 April 1974. In one of her biographies of Whitlam, Professor Jenny Hocking said of the affair: "The government's attempts to effect an additional Senate vacancy through Gair's resignation was constitutionally sound, strategically brilliant and an unmitigated political disaster".[33]

Labor was returned at the subsequent May 1974 election, though with a diminished majority in the House of Representatives, due in no small part to Joh's strong campaigning against Whitlam. In many ways Joh was now increasingly seen as the de facto conservative leader in Australia. If Joh had played a crucial part in the federal election of 1974, the state election of November 1974 in Queensland was to be a watershed moment. Calling an early poll in what was commonly thought to be a bad campaigning period, immediately prior to Christmas, Joh was able to campaign hard all across Queensland on the threats of Whitlam and the communists/socialists (they were somewhat interchangeable in his parlance) in the state ALP. Opposition Leader and fiery North Queenslander, Percy Tucker, told Joh at the campaigns outset, "I will slaughter you" and yet by the end of the campaign the ALP had lost not only its own leader's seat, but also 21 other seats, reducing it to its lowest level of representation ever – to just 11 members. Campaigning under the new National Party banner, Joh and his Coalition partners won 22 seats obtaining 59 per cent of the votes against Labor's 36 per cent (there were two independents).

In 1975 Joh had another opportunity to thwart the Whitlam Government. Queensland Labor Senator Bert Milliner died suddenly in June 1975. Consequently, Queensland Labor nominated Mal Colston as their nominee to fill the casual vacancy. It had been the convention, though not a constitutional requirement, that in such circumstances the replacement senator would be from the same party as the predecessor and that the state government would accept the nomination from the relevant party. Joh first asked for three options to be presented (as had been done on a previous occasion), but Labor refused, with Colston their only nominee. Instead of accepting this, Joh declared Colston to be a dangerous socialist and stated that rather than having to appoint the nominee of the party in question, he simply had to appoint someone who was a member of that particular party. A young Liberal MLA, David Byrne, was persuaded to enter the debate with information which he claimed "was left on my desk" that suggested Colston had been a suspect in a school arson case.[34] Colston was not charged, but on these grounds Joh deemed Colston unacceptable and appointed Albert Patrick Field to the post. Pat Field as he was known, had long Labor and union connections (almost 40 years), but was staunchly opposed to what he saw as Whitlam's immoral policies. Field was completely disowned by Labor and expelled from the ALP and therefore took his seat in the Senate as an Independent on 9 September 1975. Owing to a dispute regarding his eligibility to hold his Senate position, Field remained on leave from the Senate from October 1, having never voted, or even given his maiden speech and having only asked one question. The federal opposition refused to provide a 'pair' for Field giving them a clear majority in the Senate.

What quickly followed was the deferral of supply for the government and the Governor-General's decision to use his reserve powers to break the deadlock and sack the Whitlam Government on November 11, calling an election for 13 December. Joh campaigned vigorously against Whitlam in this election stating, "We must finish the Whitlam Government before it finishes Australia". He campaigned nationwide, enlisting the support of other non-Labor premiers. Malcolm Fraser's Liberal-National Coalition was swept to power with a 7.4 per cent swing leading to a 30-seat majority. The Coalition gained five additional seats in Queensland alone. Colston was elected as a Senator to Queensland where he remained for 21 years during which his career was described as one of "a lack of achievement".[35] In 1996 he eventually deserted the ALP amid allegation of travel rorts and nepotism and remained as an Independent until 1999 during which time he supported the Howard Coalition Government on a number of important pieces of legislation. It has been said that with the Whitlam Government losing

office in 1975, Joh lost a valuable opponent at which
to tilt:

> … the fact is that Bjelke-Petersen politically bested
> Whitlam over the 1974 Gair Affair and the 1975
> appointment of Pat Field to the Senate. Electorally,
> his campaigning was crucial in denying Labor
> control of the Senate in May 1974, and later that
> year he inflicted the worst defeat on the state ALP
> in its history.[36]

The rebirth of the Party

– from ashes to phoenix and back

The early history of the Country Party (later National
Party) in Queensland saw little tangible electoral success,
but an increasing capacity to focus in on their primary
areas of support. From World War One onwards, the
Country Party existed in a number of different guises,
drawing support from a range of rural interest groups.
In the early 1920s the Country Party was successful
in having its first federal member in Queensland
elected and as the decade closed, it won government in
Queensland (though just for one term), this time in the
guise of the Country and Progressive National Party.
This form of the party split into the Country Party
and the United Australia Party (the forerunner of the
Liberal Party) in the mid-1930s. Further attempts to

remerge these parties occurred in the late 1930s and early 1940s but failed and by the late 1940s the parties had each gone their own separate ways. Despite some further feeble attempts at remerging in the 1970s, it was not until both parties spent considerable 'time in the wilderness' after their crushing defeat in 1989 and subsequent losses in 1998 that the eventual merger to form the current Liberal National Party (LNP) was successful in 2008.

During the late 1940s and into the 1950s, the Country Party consistently won more seats than the Liberal Party, but was effectively kept out of power by the aforementioned State Labor government's engineered electoral malapportionment system. However, by the mid-1950s substantial demographic changes were beginning to undermine Labor's base, and the ALP was becoming increasingly embroiled in an internal debate about the influence of Communism in its ranks. In Queensland, this debate and other issues led to the Labor Premier Vince Gair being expelled from the ALP. He quickly formed his own party, the Queensland Labor Party (QLP) with a view to staying in office as a minority government. However, at the subsequent 1957 state election the QLP ran against the ALP in every seat, which effectively split the Labor vote. In a period of such disunity, the Country-Liberal Coalition Opposition led by Frank Nicklin won a comfortable majority (42 out of 75 seats). This success continued at the 1960 election with QLP losing 7 of its 11 seats, with Labor gaining 4 seats and with the Coalition winning overall 46 seats out of 78 seats. The Coalition subsequently won the 1960, 1963, and 1966 elections. Nicklin retired in 1968 and the premiership passed to Jack Pizzey (still under Country Party hegemony) in January 1968. However, Pizzey died suddenly in July that year and the leadership of the Country Party and thus the premiership went surprisingly to the then largely unknown, Bjelke-Petersen. Chalk, then leader of the Liberal Party and Deputy Premier held the position of premier for one week pending the Country Party's vote for a leader.

In his first election as premier in 1969 the Coalition lost 2 seats (gaining 45 out of 78) with a swing against it of just 1 per cent. At the 1972 election, the Coalition suffered a further swing of 2 per cent though it finished the poll with 2 additional seats (47 out of 82) following a redistribution which added 4 seats to the State Parliament. The changing demography of Queensland prompted the leadership of the Country Party to recognise the need to appeal to urban voters. In 1974, 8 years ahead of its federal counterparts, the Country Party became the National Party in Queensland. At the same time the National Party was professionalising its campaign capacity, adopting more modern and focused campaign tactics under the leadership of the State

Secretary Mike Evans and State President Sparkes. This saw National Party branches being formed in urban areas, especially the Brisbane metropolitan area and also in Queensland's large provincial cities with strong support from a well-funded and strategically minded central organisation. As journalist Tony Koch later observed:

> The strength of the party was its huge financial support, which enabled it to spend hugely at election campaigns. To that end, Sir Robert had overseen the establishment of the Bjelke-Petersen Foundation, a fund-raising committee of National Party luminaries who collected from business for the party coffers – and in those days, none of the details were disclosed.[37]

Political donations, particularly those of the conservative parties without a union base to fund the vast bulk of their expenditures, are a finite resource, and the aggressive and successful fundraising by the Nationals saw a concomitant falling of funding going to the Liberals. Described by William Bowe on Crikey in October 2012 as "the gold standard for Australian election massacres" the 1974 state poll saw the ALP reduced to 11 seats (famously dubbed the cricket team) with Joh campaigning strongly on an anti-Whitlam agenda to win an additional 22 seats. Swings of up to 22 per cent against the ALP saw previously 'rusted-on'

ALP seats such as Salisbury, Wynnum, Mt Isa, Ipswich West, Belmont and Baroona fall to the Coalition with many other seats considered safe also falling to the Coalition. Importantly, many of the largest swings were in regional, urban and outer urban areas, seeing previously strong Labor seats such as Albert, Mt Isa, Wynnum, Redlands and Ipswich West falling to National Party candidates – something considered impossible by virtually all political pundits. ABC psephologist Antony Green believed, "the successes of the National Party in 1983 and 1986 put Brisbane MPs in marginal seats in the National party room, not in the easy to ignore Liberal caucus".[38]

The 1977 poll saw an expected swing back to Labor with them recovering some 12 seats with a 7 per cent swing. Significantly, the Nationals not only won more seats than the Liberals, but for the first time also marginally outpolled the Liberal Party in the total number of votes, though both parties lost much of their urban foothold, the Nationals losing four seats to the Liberals' six. Nevertheless, this marked the start of the decline in Liberal Party votes and began to cause reverberations inside the party resulting in increasing instability and frustration that was to come to a head in 1983. This pressure was further exacerbated at the 1980 poll which saw two further Liberal losses to the ALP with just over a 1 per cent swing.

The October 1983 poll was held in remarkable circumstances. In August of that year, just two months before the election, a junior Liberal Minister, Terry White crossed the floor with a number of dissident Liberal backbenchers to vote against the government on a motion regarding the forming of a public accounts committee. Considered a breach of cabinet solidarity, Liberal Leader, Deputy Premier and Treasurer, Edwards sacked White, a move vociferously supported by Joh and most of White's Liberal cabinet colleagues. White then called for a spill motion declaring the leadership open. Edwards declined to nominate, and White became Liberal leader with Angus Innes his deputy. White presumed he would become Treasurer and Deputy Premier, as had been the customary practice under long standing coalition arrangements and formal agreements. However, Joh refused to accept White into cabinet on the same grounds that he had been sacked by his own leader, Edwards – namely he had broken the Westminster convention of cabinet solidarity. An impasse ensued, and the Nationals continued for a time as a minority government. Eventually, the remaining Liberal ministers resigned from Cabinet making the split in the coalition definite. Famously White then tore up a press release from Joh, a move which was interpreted by the media as White tearing up the Coalition agreement. In the following election only weeks later, the Nationals targeted conservative voters, warning of a Labor-Liberal coalition. At the same time, many Liberal branches disbanded, and their members joined the National Party in droves.

At the subsequent election in October 1983, the Nationals victory was resounding, winning 41 seats in the 82 seat parliament, just one short of a majority and gaining 38.9 per cent of the primary vote. The Liberals lost 14 seats, leaving only 8 remaining. Tellingly, there were 18 three-cornered contests and the Nationals outpolled the Liberal in 15 of them. Overall, the Nationals received a swing of 11 per cent, the ALP a swing of 2.5 per cent and the Liberals a swing of 12 per cent against. To solve his problem of a lack of a majority, Joh invited two Liberal members and former ministers, Don Lane and Brian Austin to come across to the National Party. An offer they accepted within a couple of days of the election. Joh had achieved government in his own right. It was the first time in Australian history that the National Party had formed government without being in coalition. Commentators, and those in the Liberal Party, now sitting on the cross-bench, saw this a fluke, even an aberration, that would soon be corrected at the next election. However, at the following election in 1986 saw Joh cement his position, with the Nationals picking up a further eight seats across the state. Importantly, this included some thirteen urban or outer urban seats further shoring up the Nationals' position as the dominant conservative force in Queensland. The Liberals held only nine urban seats with none north of Redcliffe, just 40 kilometres from Brisbane, except for the oddity of holding Mt Isa in far north Queensland with a popular local candidate.

The Liberal Party by now was a mere shell of its previous self, struggling to finance election campaigns and finding it increasingly difficult to attract quality candidates. Worse than this, it was, if anything, more highly focused on beating the Nationals than Labor. Academic and long-time observer of non-Labor politics, ANU academic Katharine West correctly pinpointed the Liberal problem and dilemma some years before the events of 1983 unfolded:

> In Queensland, the Liberals have often seemed to suffer from what you would call the oppressed minority syndrome. Entrapped within the coalition, the minority party has displayed a kind of love-hate relationship with its dominating partner. On the one hand the Liberals have resented the Country (now National) Party and wished to be free of it. On the other hand, they have too readily allowed their political reference point to be the National Party rather than themselves.[39]

Perhaps the greatest issue regarding the Coalition split was the loss of the Liberals in coalition and their role as a moderating influence on Joh and his plans. As in the Chalk era, with Edwards as Deputy Premier and Treasurer, there existed in Queensland politics a capacity for the Liberals to moderate, and reason with Joh, something which became less evident in the final terms of his governments. Moreover, hubris inevitably occurred, leading to future political disaster as is discussed below. By 1989, as has been discussed elsewhere in this monograph, the Nationals' fortunes had dwindled and with the loss of Joh as figurehead, the inevitable happened with a resounding Labor win. The Nationals dropped 22 seats and 24 per cent of the vote with the Liberals dropping just 2 seats, but actually suffering a 21 per cent swing. Critically for those believers in the gerrymander, the first time the Labor received in excess of 50 per cent of the vote (under supposedly gerrymandered boundaries) they resoundingly won the election. It should also be pointed out here that under 'fairer' electoral boundaries brought in by the Labor in 1989 the ALP won government with 48.7% of the vote and in 1989 maintained their grip on power with 42.9 per cent of the vote – but of course with no gerrymander!

Joh for PM

- a sad but self-inflicted end

The sad case of the 'Joh for PM campaign' highlights the inherent problem of hubris and politicians believing in their invincibility, that their rhetoric is indeed true and that they alone have the 'right stuff' to deliver their voters from evil (whatever that may be). The 1986 state election victory saw Joh at the very top of his game, having soundly defeated the ALP (down from 32 to 30 seats), leaving the Liberals with a minor increase of only 2 seats to bring their total to 10, but most importantly giving him sufficient seats to comfortably govern in his own right – 49 seats out of 89. Importantly, with the success of the National Party's strategy to build a base in urban and semi-urban seats (they now held the metropolitan centred seats of Pine Rivers, Redlands, Aspley, Greenslopes, Mansfield, Merthyr, and Springwood, as well as all of the Gold Coast and Sunshine Coast seats) it seemed that there may be a chance for the Nationals to parlay this success into a broader success nationwide. On January 1, 1987 Joh announced his bid to run for prime minister. From the start, the campaign did not really address the glaring issue that after the 1984 federal election the Nationals held only 21 of the 66 opposition seats in federal parliament. This meant that any move to have Joh as prime minister in a new government involved them winning in the order of 30 plus seats from the

Liberal and Labor parties to form a government in which they were the senior coalition partner and that Joh would then have to be elected as leader of the National Party. Understandably, most commentators correctly did not give the campaign much credence and the outcome of this quixotic tilt at the Canberra windmill was a foregone conclusion. Nevertheless, with the support and encouragement of a number of National Party stalwarts and supporters often dubbed the 'white shoe brigade' as well as from sections of the media, Joh took rapid and radical action. The Queensland National Party withdrew its 12 federal members from the federal Coalition and provoked increasingly significant fractures with the Opposition. This resulted in three cornered contests in many seats and created a perfect environment for the sitting Prime Minister, Bob Hawke, to thrive. Hawke delighted in highlighting the disunity of the Coalition and used the furore to effectively move political comment from his own government's significant shortcomings. The 'Joh for PM' (or later Joh for Canberra) campaign eventually just fizzled out like a damp firecracker. Hawke's double dissolution caught the campaign off-guard, but even without this problem, it is hard to develop a thesis where the results could have ever been much, if at all, different. The disunity caused by the whole affair cost the Opposition what should have been a chance of winning and for the ALP to make significant inroads into Queensland seats. Political journalist Paul Kelly described the belief that the 'Joh for PM campaign' could have resulted in a defeated Bob Hawke as "one of the greatest delusions ever entertained in Australian politics".[40] John Howard (then federal Opposition Leader) said that Joh was "strong on incentive but short on reality".[41]

Meanwhile, while Joh was focussing on taking Canberra, long held concerns about police corruption resulted in National Party Deputy, Bill Gunn appointing the Fitzgerald Inquiry. What was expected to be a short-term investigation became a major forensic study of not just police corruption, but of all aspects of Queensland government and public administration, and thus how the National Party governed. The Fitzgerald Inquiry began on 26 May 1987 and quickly implicated senior members of the government. Joh toughed it out for some months, but by late November 1987, after the debacle of the 'Joh for Canberra' furore, he was deposed as premier in favour of Education Minister, Mike Ahern. Joh's attempts to thwart his removal by appealing to the Queensland Governor failed. He finally announced his resignation on 1 December 1987. Joh's rapid decline was mirrored by his party. Ahern, reeling from the release of the Fitzgerald report in July 1989 was replaced in September that year, just three months out from the election, by Russell Cooper, Corrective Services and then Police Minister, who represented the more traditional National Party style leader. It was to no avail. The National Party dramatically lost 24 seats in a landslide to Labor, bringing to a close 32 years of Coalition and then National Party government.

Conclusions

This monograph takes a position on Joh well away from mainstream academic positions and usual political commentators. It specifically does this because of the paucity of authentic criticism of Joh and his governments. However, it also attempts to put Joh and his period as premier in the perspective of the wider climate of the time and of the time from which Queensland was emerging. This pre-Joh period in Queensland was highlighted largely by moribund administrations that either were found to be corrupt (like the 1930s Mungana Affair[42] and later scandals as mentioned concerning Labor administrations during the 1950s) or were simply incapable of managing the state economy to achieve positive outcomes for Queenslanders at large. It has always been easy to typify Joh as a 'hill-billy' while ignoring the fact that he was a self-made man and a successful businessman. Joh's ease of moving from his 'don't you worry about that' soundbites back into a meeting about complex state financial issues are well known to any that have worked closely with him. His oft quote line regarding 'feeding the chooks' when referring to media briefings may also explain why so many journalists are quick to jump to a negative portrayal of Joh. Too often any discussion of Joh rapidly retreats into the easy intellectual tropes of 'gerrymander' and 'corruption' as if this was something unique to Queensland and unheard of in political systems the world over. This 'safe' thinking of the left allows them to ignore their own past, patently misconstruing their own governments' shortcomings. One only has to look at union featherbedding, thuggery and a myriad of illegal actions (CFMEU, MUA, BLF, TWU, HSU – see Commonwealth's 2015 Royal Commission into Trade Union Governance and Corruption) to uncover real corruption costing businesses, state and federal governments many millions of dollars annually. And as noted earlier in this monograph, this type of corruption sees nothing built to benefit the economy at large.

The stranglehold of the unions on successive Queensland Labor governments meant that little, if any progress, was made during these periods. In many ways this paved the way for a leader such as Joh to emerge to shake things up. That he, like so many leaders, could not identify the right point at which to depart the political stage only makes him more human and not unusual.[43] Corruption is often misconstrued with the normal working of a healthy political system where government interacts with business, and business (and unions, and pressure groups) attempt to influence the government in any way they can. In the end, it is evident that Joh was a complex, hard-headed politician who understood the vagaries of the Queensland electorate perhaps better than any before or since. He undoubtedly did great things and the Queensland we see today bears an indelible and generally positive stamp from his push for development and modernisation. Sadly, the current political climate really only allows Joh-style figures on the fringes of politics, as the majority of our politicians of varying creeds, tend toward a more boring middle ground, with edges nicely smoothed by a retinue of media managers.

I believe Joh was quite well summed up in the following *Sydney Morning Herald* quote from 1986:

> He is a radical, although one of the political right, and of a strongly opportunistic kind. He cares little for political and constitutional conventions and will let nothing stand in the way of his noting of progress. His obstinacy and single-mindedness are not short comings, but a focus of strength and direction for people who badly need it.[44]

NOTES

1   Hugh Lunn, Joh -*The Life and Political Adventures of Joh Bjelke-Petersen,* University of Queensland Press, St Lucia, 1978, p 274.

2   The Queensland Country Party changed its name to National Party in April 1974.

3   Evan Whitton, *The Hillbilly Dictator: Australia's Police State,* ABC Books, Crows Nest. 1989.

4   Dean Wells, *The Wit of Whitlam,* Outback Press, Melbourne, 1976.

5   Barry Jones, "Flashback: The Psychology of the Joh Phenomenon," *Brisbane Times,* 8 August 2018.

6   Ben Smee, "Nothing has changed: Why Queensland's protest battle has raised Joh Bjelke-Petersen's ghost," theguardian.com., 1 September 2019.

7   Wayne Gilbert, General Manager, SEQEB, "Arbitration In Contempt: The Queensland Power Dispute," H R Nicholls Society, http://archive.hrnicholls.com.au/archives/vol1/vol1-2.php.

8   Ivan Gibbs, MLA, Minister for Mines and Energy, Queensland Parliamentary Debates, 26 February 1986, p. 3267.

9   Joh Bjelke-Petersen, MLA, Queensland Parliamentary Debates, 26 February 1986, p. 3266.

10 Gilbert, "Arbitration In Contempt: The Queensland Power Dispute."

11 "Bjelke-Petersen: Our home-grown banana republican," *The Age*, 25 April 2005.

12 Verity Firth, ABC News, The Drum, 14 November 2014.

13 Colin A Hughes, *The Government of Queensland*, University of Queensland Press, St Lucia, 1980, p. 83.

14 Sir Robert Sparkes, Electoral Distribution – A Question of Responsibility.

15 Paul Keating, MP, Commonwealth Parliamentary Debates, HR, 4 November 1992, p. 2549.

16 Bob Katter, MP, *Sydney Morning Herald*, 1 January 2014.

17 This program was telecast on 11 May 1987 and triggered the appointment of the Fitzgerald Inquiry later that month.

18 Phil Dickie, *The Road to Fitzgerald*, University of Queensland Press, St Lucia, 1988.

19 For a list of state royal commissions and inquiries into corruption from 1960-2005 see Prasser, Scott, *Royal Commissions and Public Inquiries in Australia*,

LexisNexis Butterworths, Sydney, 2006, Appendix 10, pp. 338-341.

[20] For details about corruption and misallocation of public finds in Western Australia see: Royal Commission into Commercial Activities of Government and Other Matters appointed in 1991 and which reported in 1992; and see Allan Peachment, (ed), *The Years of Scandal: Commissions of Inquiry in Western Australia 1991-2004*, University of Western Australia Press, Crawley, 2006; for other states but especially New South Wales see Athol Moffitt, *A Quarter to Midnight – The Australian Crisis: Organised Crime and the Decline of the Institutions of State*, Angus & Robertson, North Ryde, 1985.

[21] The correct title was Commission of Inquiry into Possible Illegal Activities and Associated Police Misconduct, Queensland was appointed in 1987 and reported in 1989.

[22] The Executive Building at 100 George Street, Brisbane, was the major building housing key government departments such as Treasury and Premier and Cabinet along with the offices of the Premier and senior ministers.

[23] For a critique of the Fitzgerald Inquiry report see Brian Toohey, "Fitzgerald – How the Process Came Unstuck," in Scott Prasser, Rae Wear, and John Nethercote, (eds), *Corruption and Reform: The Fitzgerald Vision*, University of Queensland Press, St Lucia, 1990, pp. 81-88.

24   In 1956 the Royal Commission into Allegations of Corruption Relating to Dealings and Certain Crown Leaseholds in Queensland found Labor Lands Minister, Tom Foley, guilty of soliciting party funds from graziers in return of offers for a stud lease. Foley subsequently resigned as minister and was expelled from the ALP. Criminal proceedings against him were unsuccessful. He subsequently joined the breakaway Queensland Labor Party, held his seat at the 1957 election, but lost it in 1960.

25   Brian Costar, "Sir Joh, our home-grown banana republican," *The Age*, 25 April 2005.

26   Gene Tunny, *Beautiful One Day, Broke the Next: Queensland's Public Finances since Sir Joh and Sir Leo,* Connor Court Publishing, 2018, p. 17.

27   Tunny, *Beautiful One Day,* p.18.

28   Linda Colley, "The Politics of an Apolitical Public Service," in Bradley Bowden, Simon Blackwood, Cath Rafferty, and Cameron Allen, (eds), *Work and Strife in Paradise: The History of Labour Relations in Queensland* 1859-2009, Federation Press, Annandale, 2009, pp. 163-182.

29   Colley, "The Politics of an Apolitical Public Service," pp. 163-182.

30   Colley, "The Politics of an Apolitical Public Service," pp. 163-182.

31 *The Age*, 1 January 2005.

32 Phillip Dorling, *Sydney Morning Herald*, 9 April 2013.

33 Jenny Hocking, *Gough Whitlam: His Time*, Melbourne University Press, Melbourne, 2014.

34 Craig Johnstone, "Evil friar's role was one of naivety," *Courier-Mail*, 11 November 1995.

35 "Turncoat turned into a footnote," *Sydney Morning Herald*, 26 August 2001.

36 *The Age*, 25 April 2005.

37 Tony Koch, "Joh's puppet master, Sparkes dies at 77," www.tony-koch.com, 8 August 2006.

38 Antony Green, "The Liberal-National Party – A New Model Party," abc.net.com, 30 July 2008.

39 Katharine West, RD Sherrington Memorial Dinner Address, Brisbane, 1976 as quoted in Hugh Hamilton, "Democratic Struggles in Queensland," *New Left Review*, No 65, 1978, pp. 4-11.

40 Paul Kelly, "Joh for Canberra: the false prophet," in *The End of Certainty: The Story of the 1980s*, Allen and Unwin, St Leonards, 1992, pp. 291-314.

41 Quoted in the *Courier-Mail*, 9 January 1987.

42 This concerned allegations against two former Labor premiers in the purchase of the Mungana mine. A 1930 royal commission found they had acted in collusion to profit dishonestly at the Crown's expense – see Kett H Kennedy, *The Mungana Affair,* University of Queensland, St Lucia, 1978.

43 Norman Abjorensen, *The Manner of Their Going: Prime-Ministerial Exits from Lyne to Abbott,* Australian Scholarly Publications, North Melbourne, 2015.

44 *Sydney Morning Herald,* 15 January 1986 pp. 14.

About the Author - Bruce Kingston

Bruce has some 35 years experience in management, marketing and public affairs in Australia in corporate, consulting and government roles working in various States and Territories. He was Senior Director Community Partnerships with the Great Barrier Reef Marine Park Authority co-managing Australia's largest community consultation program. He has also been a University lecturer, a Ministerial speechwriter for 2 Ministers in Bjelke-Petersen Cabinets, a political campaign consultant and a restaurateur.